Karma & Happiness

The 12 Laws of Karma That Will Change Your Life

JONATHAN REID

CONTENTS

INTRODUCTION

I want to thank you and congratulate you for reading my book, "Karma & Happiness: The 12 Natural Laws that will change your life". This book contains all you need to know about karma; what it is and how it works as well as an in-depth look at each of the 12 laws.

George Bernard Shaw once said, *"Life isn't about finding yourself. Life is about creating yourself"* and that is exactly what the universal laws of karma are about. Another great quote that sums it all up came from Ramana Maharishi, a great India saint who once said, *"whatever is destines not to happen will not happen, try as you may. Whatever is destined to happen will happen, no matter what you do to prevent it. This is certain and the best course is to remain silent".*

Those words are the keys to destiny and to karma. If you try to force something to happen, it won't. If it is meant to happen, it will. With these words in mind, take a journey back in time, back to your childhood and see how they have shaped your life. Think about decisions that you have made; did you willfully make them or were you always meant to make those decisions? We are all born into certain cultures, circumstances, a certain place on earth, poverty to wealth and with specific drawbacks, talents, and genetics. We have no power to change these things…or do we?

Karma raises more questions than anything else and karma

is more misunderstood than anyone else. Karma is a Vedic Science and has its roots firmly entrenched in India. It is the central teaching point of many different spiritual traditions, such as Jainism, Taoism, Hinduism, Buddhism, and Sikhism.

Every action, every decision we make in life happens because of actions in past lifetimes and what we do know has an effect on future lifetimes; that is the wheel of karma, linked to rebirth. Every action causes a ripple effect, like a stone does when it hits the water. These ripples affect others in untold ways and, at some point, they will come back to us. What we gain from previous actions is like an echo and you cannot escape it.

The minute you become conscious, the minute you gain access to the higher stages of enlightenment and awakening, the minute you are identified with "self" no more, that is the point at which you can leave the wheel of karma, the never-ending cure of rebirth; that is when your personal karma goes and that is the sole aim of spiritual practice.

Remember; we are all born into specific circumstances, with specific talents, drawbacks, and genes.

Welcome to the world of Karma

Thanks again for reading this book I sincerely believe there is valuable information here that truly does have the power to positively change how you life your life, I hope you enjoy it!

CHAPTER 1
WHAT IS KARMA?

"You will not be punished for your anger, you will be punished by your anger." – Buddha

The law or principle of karma is that everything in life is governed by a system known as cause and effect. You may also call it action and reaction; whichever one, it is the Principe that whatever you do, it will have a corresponding effect on the future – not just yours but all of the future. Karma is a very precise science, not the mumbo jumbo that some people believe it to be.

Karma is a universal law, or a set of 12 universal laws to be precise, in the same way that gravity is one of the laws of nature. If you were to jump off the top of a tall building, you are most likely going to die. If you hurt someone else, at some point in your life the same will happen to you. The science of karma is that everything in nature has laws to obey and obey them they do. These are natural laws, laws that are indiscriminate and impartial.

The law of karma says that whatever you sow, you will reap it but more than a hundred times over. If a tennis ball hits a wall, it has to rebound. Think of every single action that you take as a tiny seed, planted deep in the earth. Eventually, that seed is going to grow and, as it is nature, some of those seeds will flourish faster and better than others. Some will get ripe very quickly while others take decades. One thing is for sure, though; that seed will get ripe and you will be faced with the results of your actions. Your entire world, right now, is a result of actions, thoughts and words from the past.

There are two ways to describe the effects or consequences of your karma – samskaras and phalas. The phala is the result, the fruit and it can be visible or invisible It is the effect that is generally immediate or at least within your current life. The Samskaras, by direct contrast, are completely invisible effects that are produced inside of you. This is because the karma has a direct effect on your ability to be happy, or not as the case may be, in this life and in future ones. This makes karma a principle of psychology and a principle of habit. Karmic seeds or habits influence your self-perception; they create the very nature of you and, as such, affect the way you experience life.

To make that even more complicated, karma has several levels to it. There is personal karma, ancestral karma, family and societal karmas, national karma, and so you can go on. Each level will interact with the other levels. If you were to take up Yoga or Vedanta teachings, you would learn that there are three different types of karma:

- **Prarabdha karma** – the karma that you experience during your present life

- **Sancita karma** – the karma stores that are not yet at the stage of fruition

- **Agami karma** – the karma that you sow now for fruition in a future life

The science of karma teaches us that it works through the process of several rebirths. All actions, good or bad, will create an impression (samskara) or a tendency (vasana) in your mind. In time, this will result in more action that leads to more karma. The karma seeds are transported in the energy body, where the soul transmigrates. Our physical bodies are the fields where we experience the fruit of the karma and where we make more. When you hear of some religions refer to hell, it could that they are referring to a painful situation, caused by a bad action in the past.

So, why do bad things happen to people who are good and vice versa, why do good thing happen to people who are bad? Karma is just one explanation of misfortune for those who don't seem to deserve what is happening to them. Their misfortune could be down to something that happened in their previous life and, through this, we may begin to understand why, for example, in a car accident, one person may live while the rest of the car's occupants don't.

Think about this story: a mother, breastfeeding her young

baby when an earthquake hits. A pillar collapses on her, killing her outright but her child survives and is found, completely unharmed, in the rubble, still lying on his mother's breast. There can be no logical explanation for this and so many of us drive ourselves around the bend trying to figure why things happen the way they do. When you understand karma, you can stop this torture. Karma can also be used to explain child prodigies, those who are exceptional musicians or artists at a very young age, having had little or no training in their art.

Think: have you ever found yourself saying, "that's karma" or, "karma will get them in the end"? I have and I'm sure you have too. You will have had moments where you feel angry, betrayed or hurt and you may have thought to yourself, "don't get so worked up, karma will get them for you". As you begin to understand karma, you understand that isn't a devil with a big stick, there to beat you when you do something wrong as a way of evening the score up. Yes, it is a universal law but it has far more significance and is far more meaningful for your own awareness and success in life than you could ever imagine. A deeper understanding of karma can help you make the move from victim to empowerment.

CHAPTER 2
THE REAL MEANING OF KARMA

"When you think everything is someone else's fault, you will suffer a lot. When you realize that everything springs only from yourself, you will learn both peace and joy." - Dalai Lama

If you truly and deeply understand karma, you will find an awful lot falling away from you. All those negative thoughts about life, the ones that seem so repetitive, drop off when you come to realize that everything that happens to you has been caused, has been created by you. Sometime in your life, your actions dictate what is happening to you now and this should be a very sobering thought. However, it can also be a very liberating thought because it means that you have power; the power to ensure a positive life, a positive response to any situation. Don't get me wrong here; it is not about blaming yourself or about blaming anyone else. It isn't about casting judgment when a person falls ill or something bad happens to them.

Think of it more as humility, a deep understanding that, sometime in your life, you hurt someone, maybe betrayed a person, or took something from them, in a time that you have forgotten. It is all about opening up your heart to more compassion and more kindness, not just for you but for others.

Try to remind yourself of something; when someone hurts or betrays you, there is a big possibility that, at some time in the past, you hurt or betrayed them. Instead of reacting with anger, think hard and deep about the situation before you respond – don't create any more bad karma by reacting in the wrong way. I am not, by any means, endorsing weakness or telling you not to stand up for yourself; instead, I am telling you that you need to be more aware.

When you understand karma, you have a key in your hand; the key to good living. You will be able to use the laws of karma to have a successful life. For example, if you wanted to be a highly successful entrepreneur, you should help others to become the same and make sure that your help is genuinely given. This creates positive karma and then the seeds are sown for the opportunities that you help others achieve to become yours one day. If you want something in your life to be healed, you must help others to heal first. It is all about the choices you make.

While we may not always be in control of what is going in the world around us, we can be in control of our responses to what is going on. Yes, this can be incredibly challenging when you are caught up in the heat of an argument or when you have been wronged or rejected. But, the trick is in learning to stop, to be aware and to respond wisely. If you can do that, you can save yourself from a never-ending cycle of loss and hurt. It doesn't matter whether you believe in karma or not; it is already having an effect on you and the principles of karma will help you to live a much better, more successful and peaceful life.

Helpful Practices

When you look beyond karma, we have something called akarma. This is devotional practice, a practice that gives you the ultimate freedom from the tangled web of karma that has trapped you. There are practices that can help you to learn how to balance karma and to find some inner peace – two of these are Metta (Loving Kindness Meditation) and Tonglen, a Buddhist practice.

With Loving Kindness Meditation, you open up your heart to send out good wishes and prayers for every living being on earth Starting with yourself, you could pray along the lines of: "may I be happy, may I be well, may I be at peace". Then you can move on to those closest to you, your family and your friends, repeating the phrases for them and visualizing each of them in your mind as you pray. Lastly, you concentrate on someone who is giving you a difficult time; bring that person to your mind and pray for them, pray that are happy and well, that they are at peace. You can use Loving Kindness Meditation for individuals or groups of people or animals, even for the whole world if you want.

Tonglen is a lot more advanced and is also known as

"giving and receiving". It is the practice of breathing in to bring in all the pain and suffering and then breathing our healing and peace. To do this, get yourself into a quiet meditative space and connect with your feelings. Breathe in the fear, resistance, and agitation; accept what is with you, accept it with kindness and breathe out the compassion and healing for you or for all life. Tonglen is used to transmute the suffering of other people; for example, you could breathe in all the pain and suffering in war-torn countries and breathe out hope, peace, and love. When you breathe in, you hold onto a wish to remove the suffering when you breathe out you hold the wish to send happiness and comfort. These can help you to learn how to open up your heart, go beyond your own ego and discover a bigger perspective.

Thin back to the words that the Indian spirit said; think about them often and, each time, your awareness should open up a little more to help you understand the wisdom that he is conveying in his words. Take those words with on every journey – they will give you comfort and they will save you from endless hours of worry, bringing peace to your life. His words are not a call to tell you to do nothing; they are a call to action inside you, to help you learn introspection and full acceptance.

Karma means, literally, action. Think of it as the spiritual equivalent of the Low of Motion. For each action, there will be an opposite but equal reaction. In short, if you are negative in word, thought or action, expect the negativity to come straight back to you. That said, you must not see karma as a form of punishment. Instead, see it as an educational tool. How else will you learn to be a good person if you are never taught that negative and harmful actions and words are wrong? You will only suffer if you, yourself, have created the conditions for your suffering.

So, for the next few chapters, we are going to look at the 12 Laws of Karma, what they are and what they mean. Those 12 Laws are:

1. The Great Law

2. The Law of Creation

3. The Law of Humility

4. The Law of Growth

5. The Law of Responsibility

6. The Law of Connection

7. The Law of Focus

8. The Law of Giving and Hospitality

9. The Law of Here and Now

10. The Law of Change

11. The Law of Patience and Reward

12. The Law of Significance and Inspiration

CHAPTER 3
THE GREAT LAW

"As she has planted, so does she harvest; such is the field of karma" - *Sri Guru Granth Sahib*

The Great Law, known also as the Law of Cause and Effect" means that in order for you to be happy, to be at peace, to be loved and to have friends means that you must give that happiness, peace, love and friendship to others. Whatever you put out there is coming right back at you, at some time in your life.

This is the law that controls our destiny and it works on the principle that any action causes an equal and opposite reaction, which has a direct influence on our existence. Like gravity and time, karma is a universal law whose influence affects everyone. The law of physics is only applied to material objects; the law of karma is applied to every action that is performed by any living entity and it has a direct governance over the interrelations of all humans and any other living being.

Because of this, every action creates a reaction, which, in turn, creates another reaction. A never-ending chain, made up of actions and reactions, binding any living entity to their deeds, be they good or bad. This is how karma works, creating an action and the reaction at the same time, increasing the chain and keeping the performer of the action wrapped in those chains.

The action is made up of three separate components – the sense, the work, the doer. There are three motivating factors that go with this: the knowledge, the object of the knowledge and the knower. Your soul acts to bring the results of an activity and is called the doer. The instruments it uses in the actions are the senses and each action will have a different endeavor or work.

As we move from one life to the next, each living entity is determined to live life in a certain way; the reactions to the work he or she does then bind him or her in chains. When we give up on the body we are in, we move to another and then we forget our previous life. But there is no escape because of our super soul, deep within the very heart of us, sees all, it witnesses your desires of the past and it gives you the means and the directions on how to get what it was you were after. In this way, it is the soul that is reaping the results of the actions it performs.

Karma and the Bible
The holy Bible explains the universal law of karma in the statement, "As ye sow, so also shall ye reap". This is self-

explanatory and, I'm sure, is something we have all said at one time or another. When you do something, you will reap the reactions. It says that you will only reap what has been sown previously, that what is happening to you know is a result of something you did, a seed you sowed in the past. What happens to you in the future is a result of seeds that you sow now. This can be summed up in another saying that we all know; do unto others as you would have done unto you".

In short, the principle of karma is that when you perform a good action, you will receive a good reaction and, when you perform a bad action, the reaction will be bad. If you were to inflict suffering or pain on a person, you would suffer equally, be it in this life or in the next. Everything is a reaction to a past activity, and all that you are is a sum of the results of every activity you have performed up to that moment in time. If you want your life to be different as you move ahead, you must change what you do now; if you can do that, you can change the direction your life is moving in.

Say to yourself today: I am going to put this great law of karma into effect today. I will make the commitment to do the following:

1. Today, I am going to witness every choice I make in every moment. And, by witnessing every choice, I am bringing them into my conscious awareness and I will know, without a doubt, that the best way for me to prepare for any individual

moment in the future is to make sure I am fully conscious now

2. When I make any choice, I will ask two questions first – "what consequences will there be of the choice I am going to make" and "is this choice going to bring happiness and fulfillment, not just to me but to those who are also affected by the choice"?

3. Then I will ask my heart for some guidance and I will be guided by the message it gives me, be it comfort or discomfort. It is a comfortable choice, I will go ahead without any hesitation but if the choice is uncomfortable, I will stop and I will see what the consequences of my actions will be, using my inner vision. This guidance is going to help me to make the right choices spontaneously, for me and for those around me.

CHAPTER 4
THE LAW OF CREATION

In order for life to happen, your participation is required; it can't happen all by itself. Think of it this way; we are, on the inside and the outside, at one with the universe and, whatever is around you is a clue to what is inside you. So, what does all of this mean? Why is it that, although you think you have been a good person all your life, that good things just don't happen to you?

Life does not, cannot happen passively. Look at the meaning of the word, "life". It is talking about the quality that makes all living beings, animal, plant or human, different from organisms that are dead or inorganic matter. Life has chi, energy if you like – the Chinese refer to life energy as Chi – and this is attached to every living thing. If you wanted to take the meaning even further, you could ask what energy is. Energy is the power or the ability that makes things work.

Now, do you feel as though you are getting somewhere? Think about what it is in your life that you want to "work"? Do you need more support in terms of finance? Sitting on your bottom in your house, doing nothing is not giving that thought any energy! If something in life is important to you, be it your career, making new connections, a great new idea, or anything that you consider important, you have to put energy into it in order for the law of creation to come into effect. Right now, right this minute you are ready for that law to come into your life.

This is the second part of this law. As well as not being passive, you are getting involved in making things happen. You are being you and you are surrounding yourself with what you want to happen within your life.

Learn How to Meditate
And go within yourself.

What I mean by this is that you are engaging with things, with places and with people in the area that is going to affect you the most. If you decided that you wanted to learn how to meditate, how to go within yourself, you are participating in that choice, putting energy into it by making the time every day to meditate. You are making sure that you are surrounded by the choice of reading topics in the area of meditation – perhaps reflections from Buddha, joining with a local meditation group, listening to Gregorian chants, speaking with other people who are of the same mind or just reading about meditation regularly. When active participation has happened and after you have surrounded yourself with people of the same mind, then your interest in that area will come to fruition.

Pick a topic, anything that you want in your life at this moment in time; it doesn't matter what it is – money, career, relationships, hobbies, spirituality, etc. – it just must be something that you want in your life. Now the second law of karma comes into play – put the action into it, put the energy into your choice and you will be amazed at what happens.

CHAPTER 5
THE LAW OF HUMILITY

"He who speaks without modesty will find it difficult to make his words good"- Confucius

In order to change something, you have to accept it first. Humility is a good quality, an essential quality for everyone to have. It encompasses modesty and respectfulness and, across several interpretations, and in many philosophies and religious traditions, humility is a virtue being connected to transcendent unity with the divine and the universe, without an ego. Humility does not lead to weakness; it leads to strength and it is the very highest form of self-respect for a person to be able to admit to making a mistake and to then go on to make amends for that mistake.

The law of humility states that whatever you resist will persist in your life. Resistance does nothing more than feed energy into things that you don't really want. Instead of activity, sometimes you need a period of inactivity. When you allow light to shine in, then and only then will clarity come. If you do not desire something in life, it is important to slow down and ignore it; only then can you be effective in clearing out what you don't want in your life. Because you are not resisting, putting energy into something you don't want, then life will continue with ease.

You can learn an awful lot about a person who is inside of themselves by watching them, by watching what they object to strongly. The path that leads to living a life of truth takes an enormous amount of great character, a certain amount of temperance and, of course, a good dose of humility. If you want to grow to the biggest heights, you must be willing and prepared to let go, to be thankful for and to celebrate life itself. When you erase force from your spirit, inner power and morality will shine through, enough for everyone to see it. To be truly great is to have the will to stop forward movement when you really need to. True greatness is in having the ability to stop and allow insight to come through and guide you to the right balance.

One of the best examples of humility can be found in the I Ching, a great Chinese oracle system. Even though you may have an overflow of inner force, the best way to unlock that force, the power within you is to reflect had on your earthly experience, every day, and meditate on living a truthful life. There can be no greatness without rightness and, when you tap into gentle movement, even in the middle of a great force of power, harmony and peace will flow, without being disturbed, but will continue to build in small amounts.

The 34th hexagram of the I Ching is The Power of the Great – Perseverance Furthers. This hexagram points at a time when your inner worth builds with an immense force and comes into its own power. But, by that time, the strength of that power has already passed the median line and that brings its own danger - the danger that you will rely solely on your power and won't stop to ask what is right. The other danger is that you will be so intent on moving that you won't wait for the right to me to move. This is where the addition of Perseverance Furthers comes in. Perseverance is the greatest of all powers, a power that will not degenerate into nothing more than a force; a power that remains united inside you with all of the principles of justice, of what is right. When you fully understand that point, the point that justice and greatness have to be united indissolubly, you will understand the principle of humility, the true meaning or everything that happens here on earth and in heaven.

CHAPTER 6
THE LAW OF GROWTH

The law of growth states, "wherever you go, there you are". It is us who has to change, not the people, the things or the places that are around us, if we want to grow in a spiritual way. We only have ourselves and that is all that we have control over. When we can change who we are and what we are inside our hearts, our lives will follow suit and will change too.

To be fair, when you first see the Law of Growth, it can seem a little confusing to start with. But, if you take the time to think about it long and hard, it will become clear to you. When a person is unhappy, they may start to think that, if they moved house, to a new town, even to a new state far away, that their lives would change for the better. You can apply the same line of thinking to a relationship – if the partners are not happy or in accord with one another, one may think that, if the other changed something about themselves, life would be better, or if they thought and behaved the same way, they would be happier.

This is the core point of the Law of Growth. Changing where you live or how you live, trying to change the people in your life, or focusing on one, some or all of the variables that are around you will not bring about any change within you, and it certainly won't take you to the path that your soul is guiding you along. When you allow yourself to go within yourself, you will be able to identify any changes or adjustments that you know you are ready to make in what you do, how you feel and how you think.

The only thing that you have total and utter control over is you, and you alone. All of your feelings, your thoughts, and your behaviors can all be controlled by you. Only you have the ability to turn the unconscious into the conscious. You and only you can bring what is hidden in the shadows out into the light, into awareness. Changing what doesn't do you any good is a part of the path you walk in the human lifetime that you choose to come back to.

Everything we talked of above is nothing more than things. They are mere illusions of what the life you live in creates as a way of distracting you from your true path, the path to joy and peace, to knowing your true self. The truth in your heart, the acceptance and the love within your soul are the guiding lights to take you through the ages.

It is when you get stuck within these illusions and focus only what you think will bring happiness that you are changing one home for another one, one person for another, one location for another throughout your life.

The truth about and the answers of the Law of Growth are that, wherever you go, there you are. If you can fill your heart with acceptance, with joy and happiness, with tolerance, love, and peace, then that is what you will feel, regardless of who and what you are surrounded by.

CHAPTER 7
THE LAW OF RESPONSIBILITY

The Law of Responsibility dictates that if there is something wrong in your life, then there is something wrong in you. We reflect, mirror if you like, what is around us and vice versa, what is around us will mirror us. This is a universal truth and it will not change. We have to take responsibility for our own lives, for what is them, for what we do and what we say.

When you think, or feel something, when you do something, it is a reflection on the internal you. This is the same for what you hear, feel and see going on in your life. Being observant, truly seeing what goes on around you, without judging or criticizing, is what quickly puts you in touch with what goes on within you.

At times in your life, you may come across people who feel as though they are being martyred or victimized by what they see in their lives. You may have a friend that tells you they can't deal with the drama going on with the people around them. They are within a circle of people who suffer from relationships issues, financial problems or medical problems; they feel like they are drowning from all of the demands that they see being placed on them. It can be extremely stressful to find yourself in a situation like that. If a friend or a family member finds themselves in a situation where they feel life is out of their control – it could be a medical diagnosis, debt problems, an unplanned pregnancy, loss of job – you could end up feeling martyred or victimized while you try to be there for them, to support them. It isn't just stress and anxiety on the part of the person who is going through the issues but for you as well as you help them through it.

Be observant; see what is happening around you. Remember that what goes on around you mirrors what is going in within you, it reflects your own inner discontent or turmoil with something that is going on in your life. Learn to move into a peaceful state, to discover the answers to your own inner turmoil. When you can do that, those around you will move to a different place emotionally, mentally and physically.

Now is the time to start taking responsibility for the path you want to take in this lifetime. Now is the time to go within yourself and clearly see your journey. We can all do this; we all have the ability to go within and, in this lifetime, we are blessed to see clearly that which is reflected or mirrored around us and we are graced with the inner knowledge of a healing process that is yours and yours alone to take.

Be at peace with yourself and with what surrounds you as you learn to see it all clearly and your inner guidance will take you in the right direction.

CHAPTER 8
THE LAW OF CONNECTION

Even the smallest things or those that seem the least important must be done because everything that is contained within the universe is connected. Each step you take will lead to another step, and another and to get a job done, someone has to take the first step. It is important to realize and to remember that neither the first or the last step is of greater significance than any other because all steps, from the very first to the very last, are needed if a task is to be completed.

The law of connection connects all of the steps that you do or take together so that you can get the benefits of the outcome. Everything within the universe is not just connected, it is active as well and this means that your first step, the one you took to connect with what your soul wants is connected to the next step, and the one after that, and so on to the very last step until you have that outcome in your life. Each step is important to the fruition of each individual connection and that means that your past, your present, and your future are all connected in the manifestation, when it eventually comes, of your desires.

The Law of Connection connects your past life with your present life and on to your future lifetime. Many spiritualists practice regression and this allows them to clearly see every connection, be it past, present or future of the person they are regressing. In each past life, they are returning to attend to unfinished business or some other work that is revealed when their souls are reviewed. Between each lifetime, they rest and gather the strength for the next lifetime. They heal themselves, their brainwaves go into a theta state of awareness and, it is during this time that each one of them can see their next step the most clearly, the next step in the lifetime that they have chosen to live.

A person who is conscious if usually unable to see what their path in life is, what their purpose in this lifetime is. Ask them the question and they will answer, "I don't know" or "I'm really not sure". They may even tell you that they have some kind of feeling about what they should be doing but they can't figure it out. When their brainwaves enter into a theta state of awareness, it is a different matter; everything becomes clearer. The dots, the steps are all connected and they can see the steps they need to take to fulfill their destiny in this lifetime.

Many people who go through this experience tend to choose the path that is revealed to them to complete their life's work and to embrace their future. Some people will get the answers they need quickly while others will take longer. It matters not how long the journey to the answer is, only that you see it and you follow the path that is set out for you.

While there are no boundaries to where you can go, there are certain requirements that must be met. You must have sufficient spiritual energy to get from one place on to the next and you must have enough energy to take on the flesh form. When you do these things, they take the energy and these are the steps that you must connect in order to move forward on your path in life.

CHAPTER 9
THE LAW OF FOCUS

The Law of Focus says that you cannot do or think of more than one thing at a time. If you are focusing on spiritual values then it is impossible to have thoughts of anger, greed, impatience, sadness, or any other negative feeling that does nothing but create inner turmoil and upset your soul, body, and mind at the same time.

Think back to a time or times in your life where you were focused intently on something that truly interested you enough to capture your focus for every waking moment. Can you remember how often you found yourself sidetracked away from it, thinking about troubled times or feelings? Most likely, it didn't happen because, when you are completely focused on a thing, there is no room for anything else. When you had children, most likely you were so focused on them, on their wellbeing and on providing for them, nurturing them, that nothing else got a look in. You would not have had the time, the energy or the interest to focus on anything else.

How many of you have written and published a book? A few of you, I would imagine, even just publishing for Kindle on the Amazon store. Think back to when you wrote that book. Did you set time aside each day or week to write it? And during your writing time, were you so focused on what you were doing that nothing else distracted you? Taking the decision to focus on spiritual values is no different because you are still focusing on one thing, leaving you no room, time or energy for anything else. You still need to set aside time for meditation, just as you did when you wrote a book or did something else that required all of your focus.

Life won't stop, the world won't stop turning because your focus is on something else. You will still continue to go about your daily life and you will still have to deal with the things that happen, like your car breaking down, a sick child or the washing machine giving up the ghost but when you are focusing on spiritual values, there is a kind of veil between you and the stress of life; it can't touch you while you are focused on something else. It is almost like you become an observer, someone who is not involved in the moment, merely watching.

There is another part to the Law of Focus and that is that whatever you think about will expand; if you focus on something positive, your mind will follow and go in a direction that is positive, your inner voice will become positive and your life will begin to improve.

Focus gives you incredible power over your mind – when you train your focus on something, your mind is forced to turn in that direction. If you focus on that thought or feeling for a minute, your mind will follow it for a minute. Learn how to consistently focus for weeks and months and your life will start to move in that direction. In short, when you focus your mind, it expands to your life.

It is not possible for me to say how long it will be before a positive focus has the positive effect on your life. However, it will happen eventually, you just need to maintain your focus and not get sidetracked. If you don't see results in a few days or a week, don't give up because it will happen. If you are constantly struggling with limiting or negative thoughts, keep in mind that this law is immutable; it will never fail you. It doesn't matter how down you may be or how discouraged you are about a situation, the law of focus will always deliver.

CHAPTER 10
THE LAW OF GIVING & HOSPITALITY

The Law of Giving and Hospitality is the 8th law of karma and it says that, if you believe that something is true, at some point in your life you will be asked to demonstrate the truth you believe in. This is where you get to determine if your thoughts and your behaviors match up with one another. This is where you get to determine if the words you speak are in accord with your actions and your thoughts.

Let me give you an example, from a man who does past life regression. He says that, after listening to messages from his clients, after hearing those clients speak to life masters between lifetimes, he believed that he could get his own life messages from the same masters. This pushed him into meditating daily and developing a method that allowed him to go within himself. With true determination, he finally succeeded and heard his own message from the masters. From then on, the messages became more frequent.

Of course, I'm not for one minute suggesting that this should be your belief. The basics of the law state that, whatever you truly believe, one day you will be asked to put into practice. Or, put in another way, whatever you have learned during your time and whatever you have received, you will have to return it at some point in your life. The opportunity will arise, the right time will come along, you just need to look for it.

Think of this in terms of lessons you have learned throughout life; one day, you will be asked to demonstrate that you have learned them and you will be asked to use your knowledge to give back those lessons to someone else. Think about times when you have received help from someone – it doesn't have to be a physical help, like a loan of money or a car, or anything like that. It can be anything. One day, you will be asked to return that help, to return that kindness to someone else.

If you cannot demonstrate the truth you say you believe in, then it shows that you do not truly believe in it. In order to provide and to give hospitality, you must be able to practice your belief in providing and in giving hospitality. If you provide nothing more than hostility and emptiness then it says that you believe others to be hostile and empty and this will reflect back on you, to show your own hostility and emptiness.

Remember – the core to all belief is a kindness. If you don't have that, you don't have true belief.

CHAPTER 11
THE LAW OF HERE & NOW

This is quite a simple law – in short, you cannot possibly be in the here and now if you are constantly looking back to the past to see what happened, or looking forward to the future to see what may be. Your old thought patterns, your old dreams, and your old behavior patterns are stopping you from creating new ones in the present. Have you ever said to anyone, "stop living in the past" or has anyone ever said it to you? Think hard about it – if you do spend a lot of time delving into the past, do you find that things in your present life don't go to plan, your life doesn't move forward like it should?

There is always a time for reflection on the past and that time is to look back at old behavior patterns, identify them and create awareness of them – so you don't repeat them. In this way, you can bring a healthy closure to those areas.

The real problems happen when people choose to look backward for no particular reason and they take no action to create healing of past behaviors. What happens then is that you become full of anger, regret, and sadness. Sometimes, you will even find yourself with feelings of inertia and that leaves you with no energy for being in the here and now.

Your mind, your body and your soul can become stuck in the past. You may be thinking back to old relationships, trying to work out what went wrong. You could be replaying old conversations, thinking back to events that happened. You may be thinking back to past illnesses, deaths in the family or amongst your friends or anything else that may have happened in the past. When you go back to these but do not process them, do not take any action to heal them, your spiritual, physical and mental energies are dragged back to a time and a place that was unhealthy. If you stay there, if you continue to stay with these old issues, you cannot grow. You cannot create any new and healthy behaviors, thoughts and feelings.

There are lots of ways to close down the past, especially with things that still take your attention away from the here and now. You can use regression or hypnosis techniques – but do only use registered and professional therapists to do this with. Both are excellent ways to bring closure to the past. There are other good ways – Reiki, aura cleansing, chakras, EFT techniques – all will help you to bring peace to your life and close the past down. And of course, the very best way is meditation.

To learn to go inside yourself is a way of giving yourself the gift of hearing the messages from your soul. You can have free access to direction, wisdom, and guidance every day.

Just keep these words in mind – the past should stay where it is, in the past. You can't change the past and you can't change the future. The past has shaped you into what you are and the here and now will shape your future. The here and now is all that matters.

CHAPTER 12
THE LAW OF CHANGE

The Law of Change states that history will continue to repeat itself until you learn what needs to be done to change your path. We all know that change is inevitable and, for all of us, it is an essential part of life. If you do not take the steps to change, be it yourself or things in your life, then history is going to repeat itself, over and over, until you learn the lesson.

Let's go back to a terrible and fateful day in September 2001. We all remember the horror of 9/11; we all remember the shock, the feelings of terror, sadness, and anger as we watched those planes fly into the twin towers. But think on, in the 15 years since that day, has anything changed? Is the world more at peace than it was then? Do you think there is more tolerance in the world? More compassion, more acceptance and more love for our fellow human beings, regardless of their nationality, race or religious beliefs? Many reading this would be shaking their heads emphatically right now and saying, quite clearly, no, there has been no change. Yet, others will be saying the opposite, that they see it from a different perspective. And perspective is what it all comes down to, more often than not.

If your heart is a peaceful one, a loving and a compassionate one then that is how you will see life. If you are full of anger, greed, resentment or intolerance then that is how you will see everything around you. Now is the time to make some choices. Choose to see the good in everyone, choose to love everyone, whether they are angry or filled with darkness. Choose to be compassionate, send positive energy and unconditional love to surround these people; do this and gradually the vibrations of negativity will turn to positivity, to lightness.

Choose to not want history to repeat itself. Make changes in your own life to give unconditional love to all who cross in front of you. Stop watching the news, stop reading the papers and stop believing that all of the sensationalism is true. Choose to meditate every day, to go within yourself every day and choose not to let history repeat itself, to learn from lessons and change.

This is pivotal law in a lot of different respects. While you may not be able to control history repeating itself in terms of attacks like 9/11, you can choose to change things in your life to stop it from happening. Look at your life, your relationships, everything you do. Are there patterns there?

Do bad or unhelpful things keep happening to you? Look at your patterns of behavior and see where you can make changes to stop it from happening again. Make the decision today that you have learned your lessons and are going to change your path in life.

CHAPTER 13
THE LAW OF PATIENCE & REWARD

The Law of Patience and Reward says that to receive a reward you must put in the initial work and be patient in waiting for the reward. If you want rewards of a lasting value, then you must be patient and work persistently towards them. The true joy isn't in doing something for immediate reward; it is in doing what you were supposed to do, with the knowledge that the reward will come along in good time.

This is a challenging law for many people because it involves having to be patient. In our current times of instant gratification and being able to get what we want when we want it, patience is fast becoming very difficult for people to practice.

Cast your mind back to the 2nd law, the Law of Creation; it

is very similar to this one in that it says that if you are to make things happen in your life you must be prepared to participate in making them happen. For most people, the most unsettling feeling is the one of uncertainty. Most people don't know what they truly want; they don't know what path to take to feel comfortable with the choices they make. They don't really know what they want out of a relationship, what would fulfill their passions. They don't even really know what career path would ensure that they start the day with joy. They cannot see what feeds their souls.

Without knowing all of this, many feel unmotivated to put in the work to get the rewards and, more often than not, patience certainly doesn't factor into the process. Think back to when you last had a very clear goal in your mind. A goal that made you excited at the prospect of attaining it. Thin about how it made you feel, the effect that it had on you.

This is key to the Law of Patience and Reward. When you decide what you are going to do, how you are going to do it, then the joy will follow that. That is when the patience will come in, the patience to do what you need to do and wait for when the rewards of your work come in. This is part 2 of this law – you must have the ability to let the rewards come in their own time. You must have belief in the process and trust in the outcome.

We have but one journey in life – to find the path that leads you to feel full of energy and passion as you follow it, to allow the process to unfold as it should, in its own time.

When you have that patience and you put in the work then you must trust that all will happen as it should, when it should. When you can do this, this is a fantastic law.

CHAPTER 14
THE LAW OF SIGNIFICANCE & INSPIRATION

The Law of Significance and Inspirations states that you will get back whatever you put into something. For every contribution you make to something is a contribution to the whole thing and the real value of anything is the result of the energy that you have put into it.

Karma is a lifestyle; it promotes positive actions and positive thinking and it also employs the act of self-reflection in order to fix problems in your life. This law has already been referred to in several of the other laws, in some way or other. But this is a specific law that focuses on the energy and the intent that you put into something.

Whenever you make a contribution towards something, towards the whole, an impact is created. That starts off a ripple effect that you may never see the end of. Trust me on this, though; your soul will know what the end result is; your soul creates the good intentions, provides the support and the enlightenment.

Only you can begin the process of creating inspiration and significance that spreads to everyone around you, touching everyone with purity and goodness. Your soul will feel it and will communicate it within you through joyful feelings, feelings of love and an intuition inside of you. It is your soul that hears the voice that guides and follows it to manifest universal inspiration.

The Law of Significance and Inspiration is an important one for everyone to learn. When you apply intent and energy to something you will receive the value of that intent and energy but you do not do this alone – you are a part of a whole, just one person making a contribution, an important one, to the greater good and this was summed up nicely in the Bible.

It says "two are better than one because they have a good return for their work. If one falls the other helps him up. Pity the one who falls but doesn't have anyone to pick him up. One can be overpowered while two can defend themselves and each other". Ecclesiastes 4:9-12

One is a small number, too small to achieve greatness but your contribution to the whole is an important one, a part of the whole and you will receive the value that is directly proportionate to what you put in.

BONUS
10 WAYS TO IMPROVE KARMA

Buddhism states that karma is the bad or the good circumstances that come from an action previously performed and many people ask how they can improve their karma. Strictly speaking, karma cannot be improved, it can only be healed. Bad karma can be seen as things that happened in the past, things that have not gone through closure or been resolved. These situations are normally of an emotional or a spiritual nature.

Karma will continually come into new situations in the present but this will be of the same type as the original situations that were unsolved and this just makes you feel the same old emotions over and over again. You will feel as though you are living a type of Groundhog Day, the same life over again, the same circumstances, as you are trapped in a vicious cycle.

Karma is there to teach you lessons, things that you wanted to learn on a spiritual level even though some situations are challenging and can be difficult, even impossible at times but that is the very nature of karma. So how do you heal karma?

1. Go back to situations, feel them. This may not always be easy and many resist it because it can be painful

2. Handle the situation, process it so that you can gain some closure. This can involve many things – forgiveness, acceptance, facing the situation head on instead of running away, making a new decision or just moving on. Whatever needs to be done must be done to heal your karma

There are things that you can do to help "improve" your karma though and here they are. These are things that you should practice regularly:

1. **Repeat Actions**
If you repeat something over and over again, you will release karma and it will go out into the world. This works for good and bad situations so if you were to continually lie, cheat, steal, deliberately hurt others you will create bad karma. Be very aware of your actions; learn to develop better habits and your karma will improve over time.

2. **Chant**
Chanting is an incredibly powerful thing to do. It can help

to clear your mind, body, and soul of negative patterns of karma and can help you to get on the path for good karma. One of the best chants is the Compassionate Buddha Mantra – in order to experience peace, joy and tranquility, simply close your eyes and chant "om mani padme hum."

3. **Volunteer**

It doesn't just feel good to help other people, it gives your karma a real boost of positivity. Always be on the lookout for ways that you can help someone, be it on a large or a small scale.

4. **No Audience**

All good deeds are recognized so forget about needing an audience to perform yours – you don't need one because karma will give you the nod.

5. **Listen**

You may hear what someone is saying to you but do you actually listen properly? Make sure you do and be the person that people come to when they need a friendly ear or a shoulder.

6. **Express Love**

Love is another incredibly powerful emotion, particularly when it comes to good karma. Make sure you practice self-love and love others unconditionally, without any judgement.

7. **Patience**

Patience is a real virtue and is something many of us are lacking in. When you are impatient you can easily become angry at others. Learn patience and you will find that you are more relaxed, you can think more clearly and your actions are more appropriate.

8. Forgive
When you hold a grudge against someone, it causes blockages. Learn to let go, to forgive people and those blockages will go, allowing the good karma to flow once again.

9. Be Grateful
Every night, write down all of the things that you are grateful for from that day. It may be something big, or it may be something very small; write it all down and express that gratitude.

10. Stronger Spirituality
No matter what your beliefs are, look for a spiritual guide who can take you to better karma. Expand your vision and learn from those who know.

CONCLUSION

Thank you again for purchasing this book! I hope that you now more aware of what karma is, of what it means and how it works in your life and that of others. You may, for a while, find yourself consciously aware of everything that you do, everything that you say, wondering what effect it will have on karma.

The most important thing to remember is this: what goes around, comes around. Whatever you do now will come back to you, whether in this life or the next one or the one after that; it will come back.

If you have found this book useful, you might want to consider going further and getting in touch with a spiritual group that can help you to further your understanding of karma, of how to control your own life.

Finally, if you enjoyed this book, then I'd like to ask you for a favor, would you be kind enough to leave a review for this book on Amazon? It'd be greatly appreciated!

Thank you and good luck on your journey through your new life.

Printed in Great Britain
by Amazon